ARMORED REPTILES

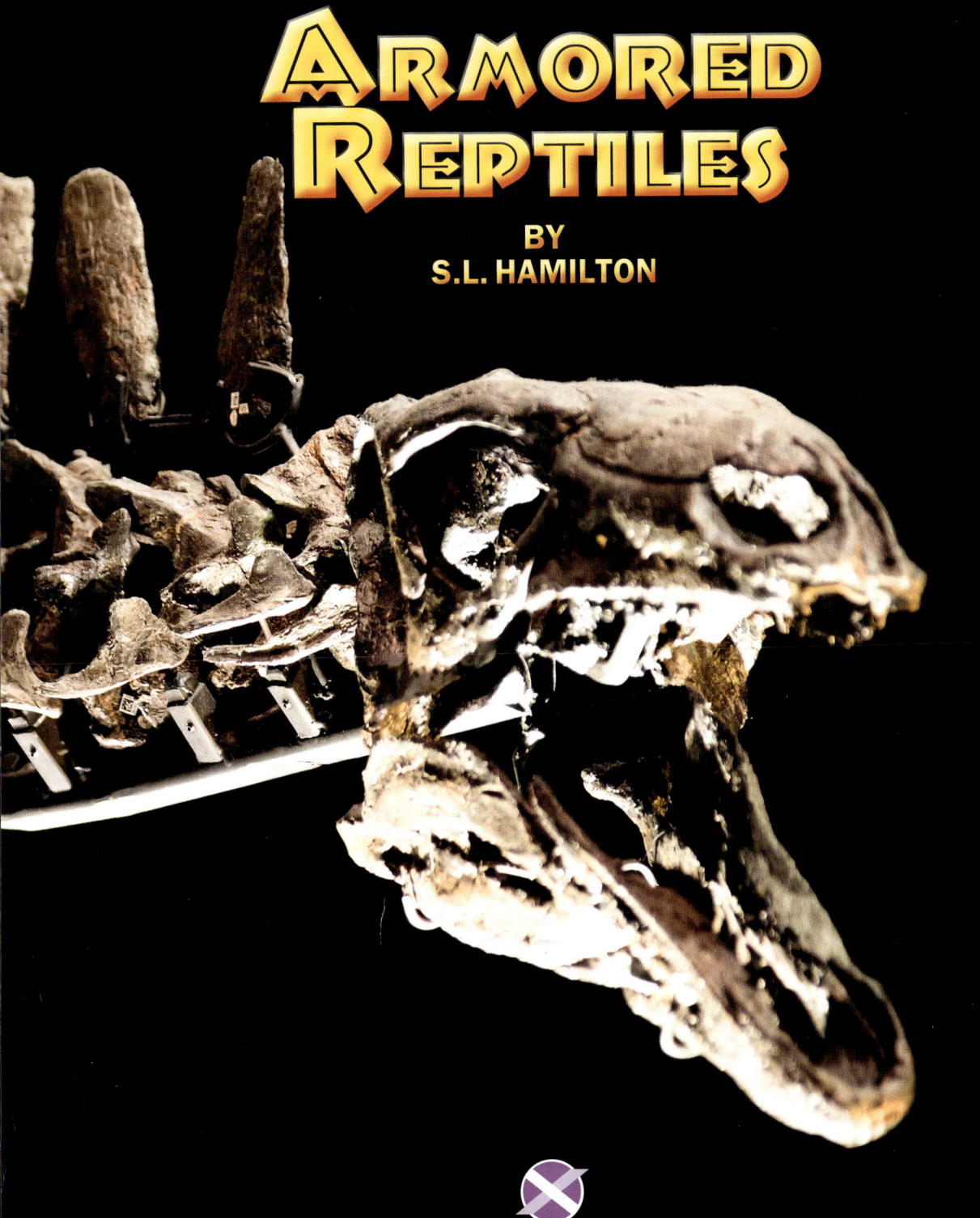

BY
S.L. HAMILTON

A&D Xtreme
An imprint of Abdo Publishing | abdopublishing.com

abdopublishing.com

Published by Abdo Publishing, a division of ABDO, PO Box 398166, Minneapolis, Minnesota 55439. Copyright ©2018 by Abdo Consulting Group, Inc. International copyrights reserved in all countries. No part of this book may be reproduced in any form without written permission from the publisher. A&D Xtreme™ is a trademark and logo of Abdo Publishing.

Printed in the United States of America, North Mankato, MN.
092017
012018

THIS BOOK CONTAINS RECYCLED MATERIALS

Editor: John Hamilton
Graphic Design: Sue Hamilton
Cover Design: Candice Keimig and Pakou Vang
Cover Photo: iStock
Interior Photos & Illustrations: Alamy-pgs 4-5, 10-11, 14-15, 18-19, 22-23, 24-25, 26-27, 28-29, 30-31 & 32; AP-pg 21 (inset); Gary Larson-The Far Side-Thagomizer comic-pg 11 (inset); Getty Images-pg 13 (inset); Glow Images-pgs 8-9; iStock-pgs 1, 12-13, 20-21 & 24 (inset); Science Source-pgs 6-7 & 17; Shutterstock-pgs 2-3, 10 (inset) & 16

Publisher's Cataloging-in-Publication Data

Names: Hamilton, S.L., author.
Title: Armored reptiles / by S.L. Hamilton.
Description: Minneapolis, Minnesota : Abdo Publishing, 2018. | Series: Xtreme Dinosaurs |
    Includes online resources and index.
Identifiers: LCCN 2017946541 | ISBN 9781532112928 (lib.bdg.) | ISBN 9781532150784 (ebook)
Subjects: LCSH: Ornithischia--Juvenile literature. | Prehistoric animals--Juvenile literature. | Dinosaurs--Juvenile literature. | Paleontology--Juvenile literature.
Classification: DDC 567.915--dc23
LC record available at https://lccn.loc.gov/2017946541

Contents

Armored Reptiles 4
Types 6
Tails 10
Heads 14
Teeth 16
Largest Armored Reptiles 18
Smallest Armored Reptiles 22
Most Unusual Armored Reptiles 24
Nesting 26
Extinction 28
Glossary 30
Online Resources 31
Index 32

Armored Reptiles

Armored reptiles lived 165 to 145 million years ago, during the Jurassic and Cretaceous periods. Also known as Thyreophorans, or "shield bearers," these dinosaurs carried weapons on their bodies.

Euoplocephalus
(Well-Armed Head)

From bony clubs and spikes to body armor, these fierce plant eaters boldly protected themselves against hungry predators.

Types

Armored reptiles are divided into two groups: ankylosaurs and stegosaurs. Ankylosaurs had plates of body armor covering nearly all of their bodies. These bony plates, or scutes, extended across the dinosaur from head to toe.

XTREME FACT – *Euoplocephalus* was the most armored ankylosaur. It even had armored eyelids. However, ankylosaurs did not have armor on their bellies. It was their weak point.

Stegosaurs had plates and spikes running in rows down their bodies. The pointy plates, or scutes, were as tall as 2.5 feet (.76 m). They were made of a bony material called osteoderm.

The plates likely acted as protection, but were not very strong. They made the dinosaurs look bigger and tougher than they really were. The plates also helped attract mates.

XTREME FACT – Male and female stegosaur plates may have been shaped differently. Scientists guess that females had sharper, pointier plates to defend against predators. Males had bigger, wider plates to attract females.

TAILS

Armored dinosaurs had vicious weapons on their tails. Stegosaur tails ended in four sharp spikes. The spikes probably faced sideways, not up.

A puncture wound matching the shape of a stegosaur tail spike was found in a fossilized bone of an *Allosaurus*, a carnivore that ate stegosaurs. This proved that armored reptiles' tails were used in combat.

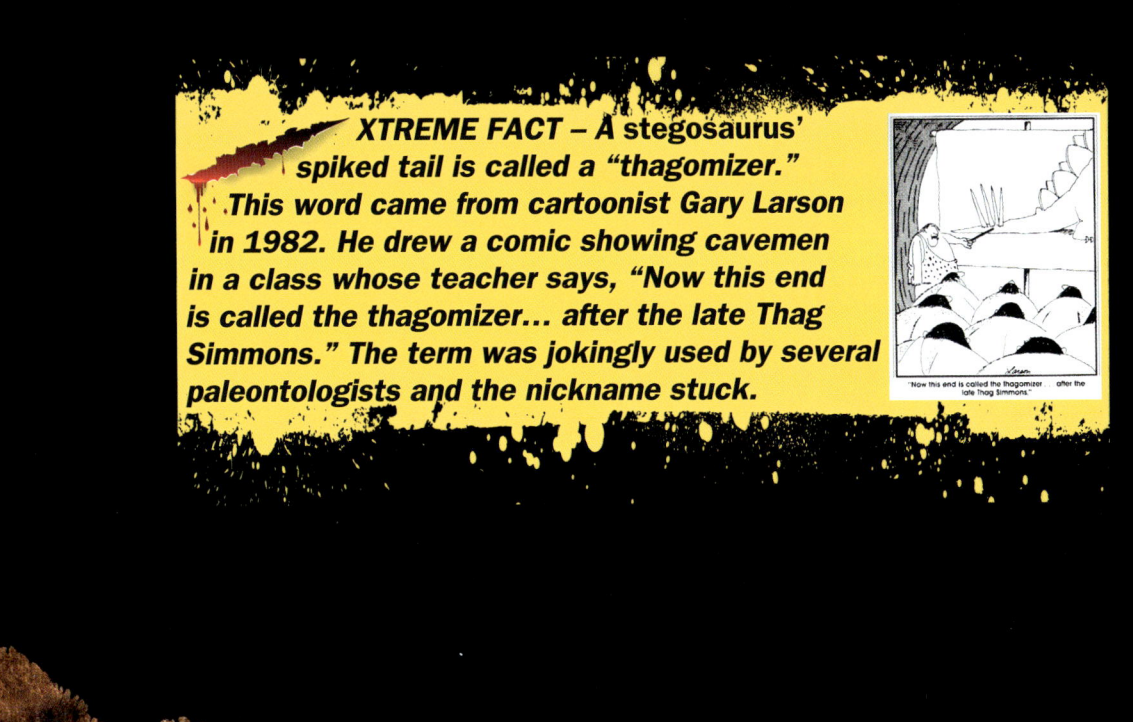

XTREME FACT – A stegosaurus' spiked tail is called a "thagomizer." This word came from cartoonist Gary Larson in 1982. He drew a comic showing cavemen in a class whose teacher says, "Now this end is called the thagomizer... after the late Thag Simmons." The term was jokingly used by several paleontologists and the nickname stuck.

11

Ankylosaurs had a tail made of tightly packed bones that locked together. At the end of the tail was a final rocklike ball of bone. The muscular tail could swing from side to side in a 100 degree arc.

ANKYLOSAUR TAIL CLUB ARC

100 Degree Arc

TAIL CLUB

Knob

Handle

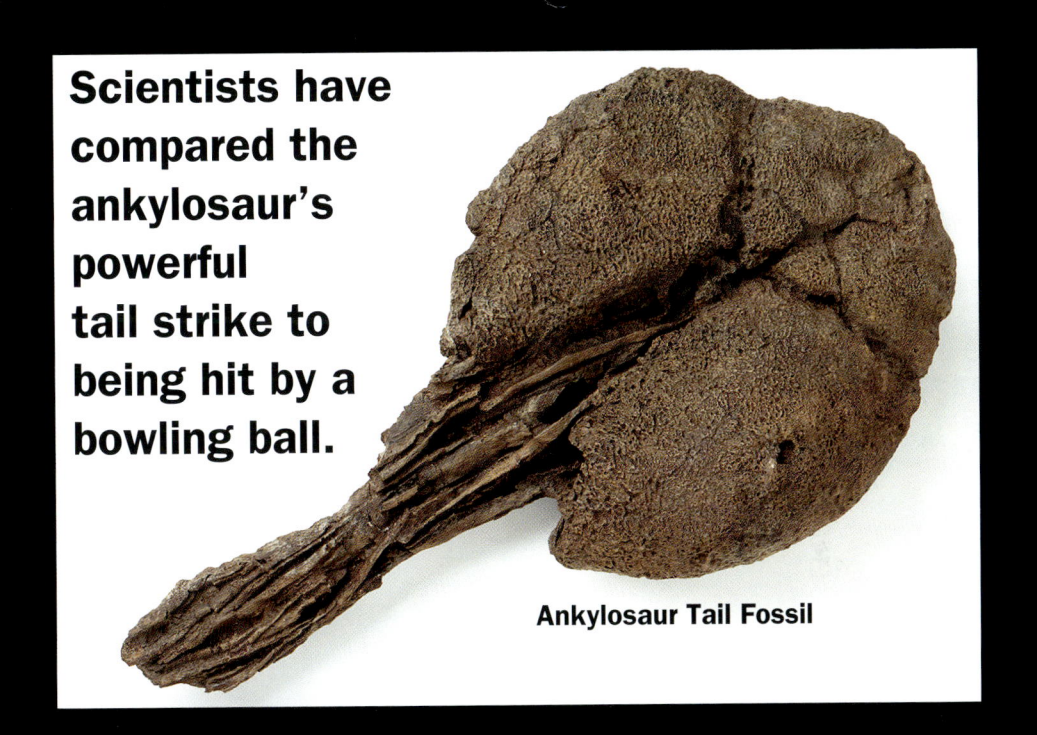

Scientists have compared the ankylosaur's powerful tail strike to being hit by a bowling ball.

Ankylosaur Tail Fossil

13

HEADS

Armored reptiles had some of the tiniest heads, compared to their body size, of any dinosaur. Scientists believe their brains were no bigger than a dog's brain.

Armored reptiles had simple lives. Their brains fulfilled their needs for finding food, protecting themselves, and reproducing.

Teeth

Armored reptiles were plant eaters, or herbivores. Stegosaurs had small, peg-like teeth with jaws that could move up and down to chew. Like cows, they may have stored food in their cheeks to give them time to completely chew before swallowing.

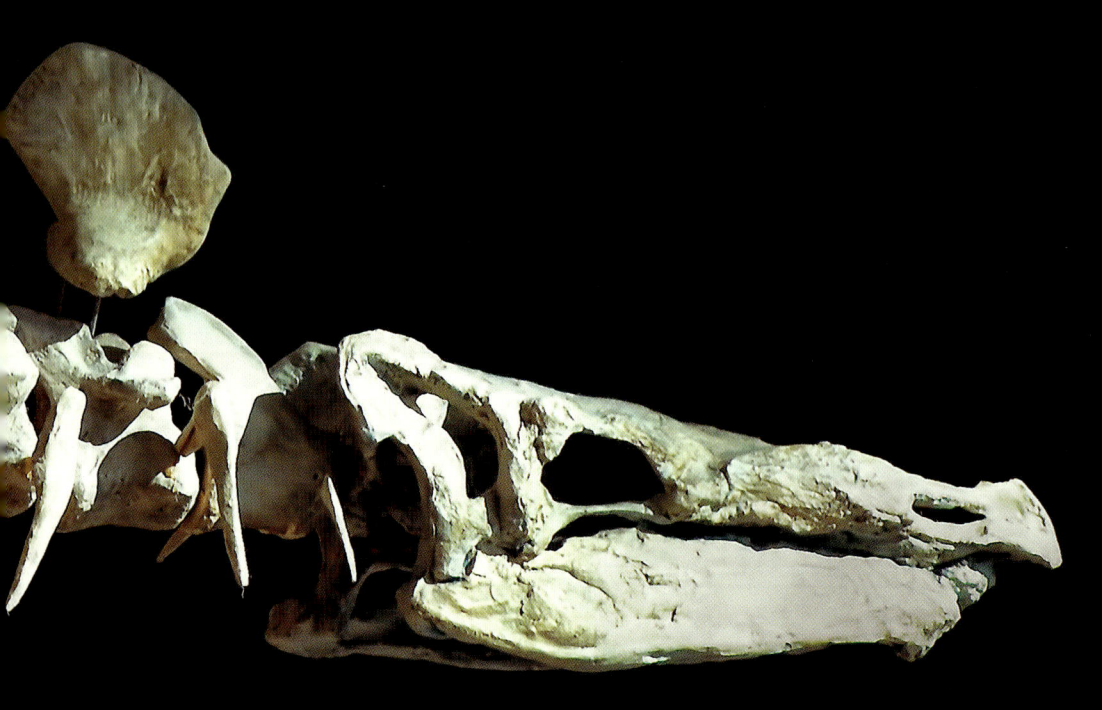

Stegosaurs had a beak in front, but no front teeth.

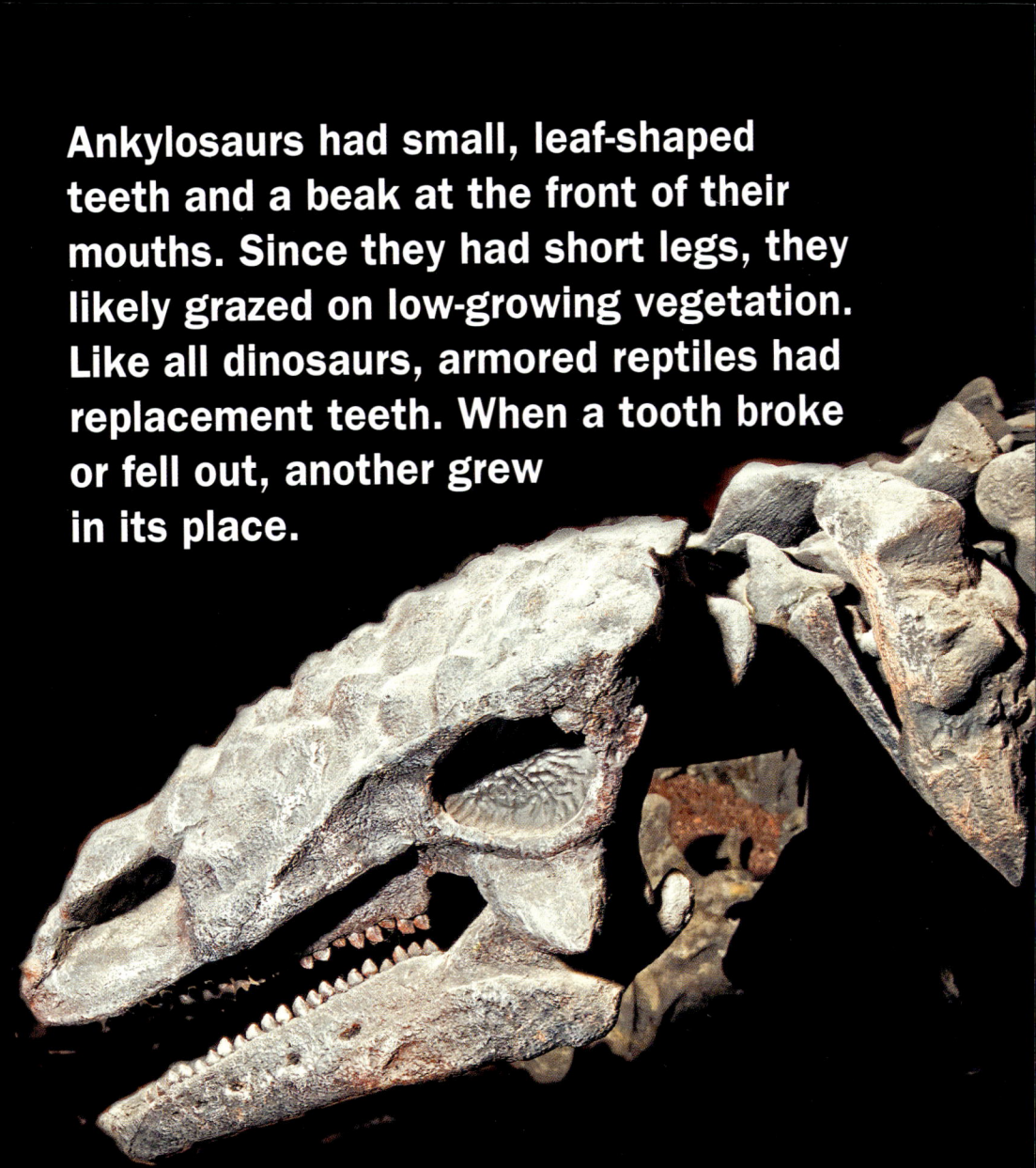

Ankylosaurs had small, leaf-shaped teeth and a beak at the front of their mouths. Since they had short legs, they likely grazed on low-growing vegetation. Like all dinosaurs, armored reptiles had replacement teeth. When a tooth broke or fell out, another grew in its place.

XTREME FACT – Because replacement teeth took a long time to grow in, ankylosaurs probably used their muscular tongues to help them eat.

Largest Armored Reptiles

Stegosaurus was the biggest armored reptile, living 155.7 to 150.8 million years ago. It grew to a length of 30 feet (9 m). It weighed as much as 5 tons (4.5 metric tons). The name *Stegosaurus* means "roof lizard." When the fossils were first found, it was thought that the plates laid over the dinosaur like tiles on a roof.

XTREME FACT – Because *Stegosaurus* had such a small brain, scientists once thought it had a second brain near its back legs that controlled its weaponized tail. This idea has since been rejected.

Ankylosaurus lived in North America 68 to 66 million years ago. This huge armored reptile grew to 25 feet (7.6 m) long and weighed as much as 7.5 tons (6.8 metric tons). It is described as a "living tank."

Ankylosaurus
(Great Belly)

The armored body and weaponized tail made *Ankylosaurus* difficult to attack. Even its overall wide, flat shape stopped predators from grabbing or biting it. Because of this, it was one of the last dinosaurs to become extinct.

XTREME FACT – The earliest ankylosaurs were called nodosaurs. They had not yet developed the bony club at the end of their tails. Edmontonia *is an example.*

Smallest Armored Reptiles

Scutellosaurus was one of the smallest and earliest-known armored reptiles. It grew to only 4 feet (1.2 m) long and weighed about 22 pounds (10 kg). The early stegosaur was covered with the bony scutes and spiked plates that helped protect all the armored reptiles from predators.

Scutellosaurus, whose name means "little shield lizard," lived 200 to 176 million years ago in North America. Unlike its future cousins, it may have walked on two feet. Its long tail kept the small dinosaur balanced.

A Scutellosaurus *pack is attacked by a much larger predator.*

Gargoyle Statue

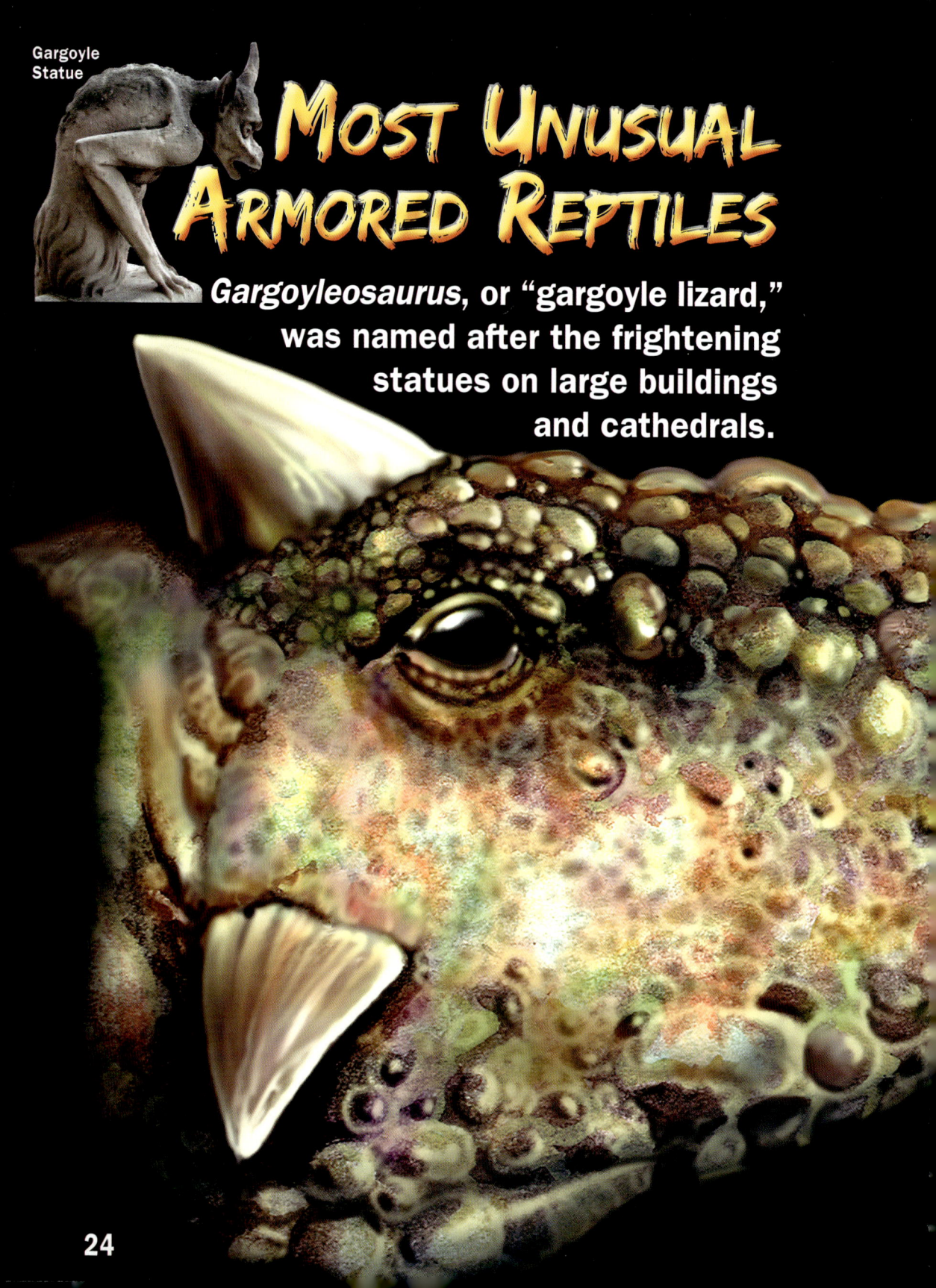

Most Unusual Armored Reptiles

Gargoyleosaurus, or "gargoyle lizard," was named after the frightening statues on large buildings and cathedrals.

24

Gargoyleosaurus was one of the earliest ankylosaurs, living 154 to 142 million years ago in today's North America. It grew to a length of 13 feet (4 m) and weighed about 2,200 pounds (998 kg). Unlike others of its kind, *Gargoyleosaurus* had hollow armored plates covering its body. Future ankylosaurs had solid plates of bone protecting them.

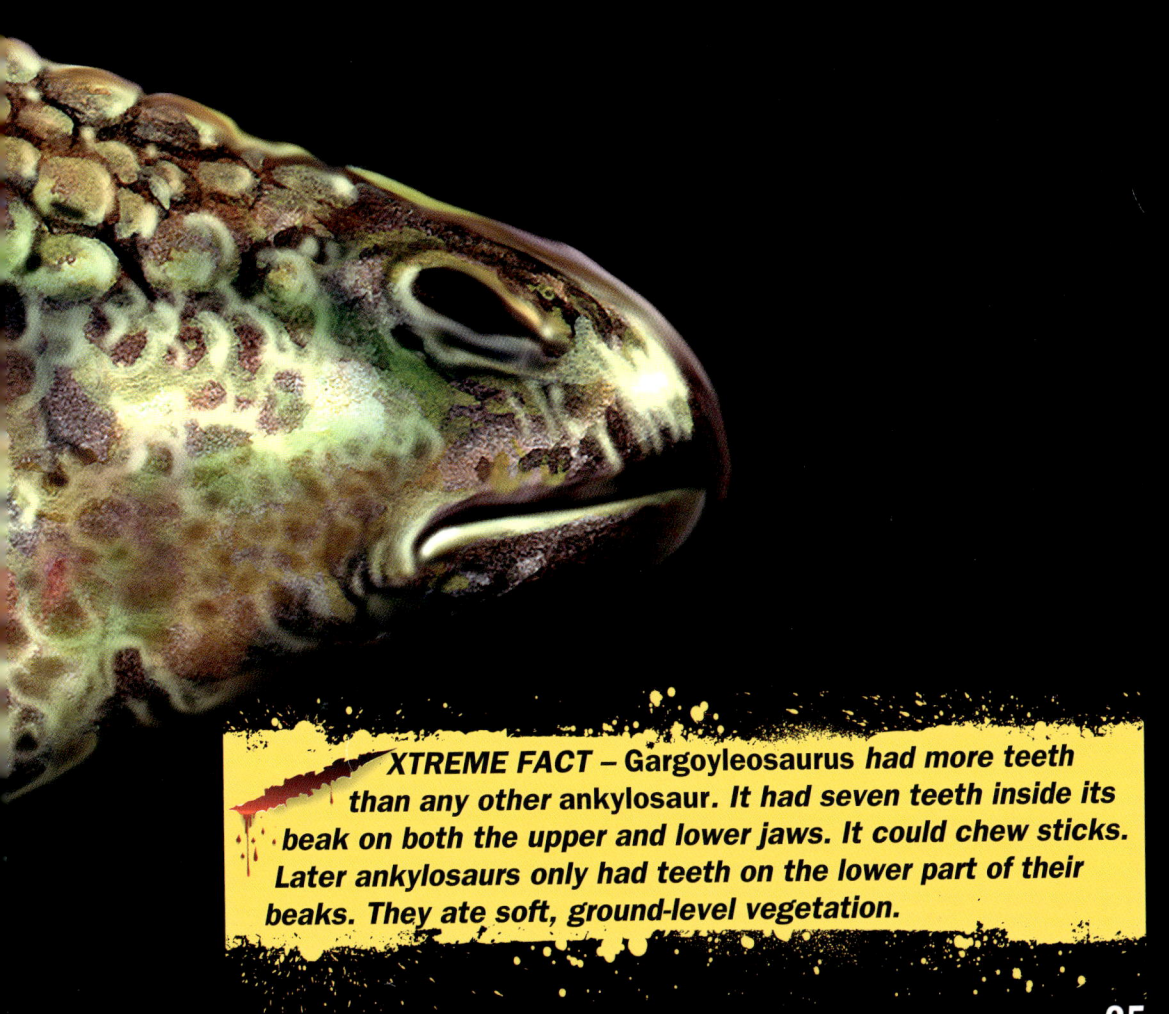

XTREME FACT – *Gargoyleosaurus had more teeth than any other ankylosaur. It had seven teeth inside its beak on both the upper and lower jaws. It could chew sticks. Later ankylosaurs only had teeth on the lower part of their beaks. They ate soft, ground-level vegetation.*

Nesting

No fossil nests have been found that could be positively identified as belonging to an armored reptile. However, paleontologists believe that dinosaurs laid eggs in above-ground nests. Armored reptile families may have lived in herds and stayed with their offspring. Living as a group would have given the dinosaurs additional protection against large predators.

XTREME FACT – Researchers at a fossil site known as the Morrison Formation, in the states of Wyoming and Colorado, found 80 Stegosaurus fossils all in one area. This seems to prove that some armored reptiles lived in groups.

27

Extinction

About 66 million years ago, a world-changing event occurred. It may have been an asteroid striking the Earth. Perhaps volcanoes began erupting. Climate may have changed. Diseases may have struck. Perhaps it was a number of things that caused the extinction of dinosaurs.

Ankylosaurs were one of the last dinosaurs to die out. Their great armor protected them from predators, but couldn't stop their extinction. Scientists continue to look for clues to explain what killed these tough prehistoric creatures.

GLOSSARY

CARNIVORE
A creature that eats meat in order to survive.

CRETACEOUS PERIOD
A time in Earth's history from about 144 to 65 million years ago. At the end of this period, a world-changing event occurred and all the dinosaurs died.

EXTINCT
When every member of a specific living thing has died. Armored dinosaurs are extinct.

FOSSILS
The preserved remains or imprints of prehistoric animals or plants in stone.

HERBIVORE
Animals that eat plants as food.

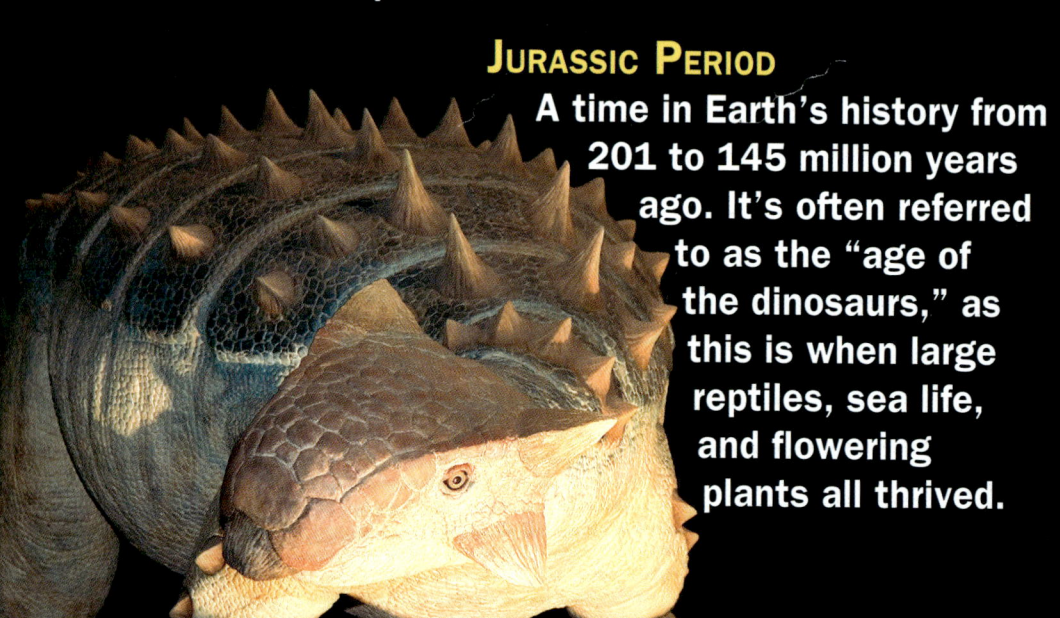

JURASSIC PERIOD
A time in Earth's history from 201 to 145 million years ago. It's often referred to as the "age of the dinosaurs," as this is when large reptiles, sea life, and flowering plants all thrived.

Osteoderm
Bony plates that form on the skin for protection. It was found on armored reptiles, as well as some of today's lizards, crocodiles, and frogs.

Paleontologist
A person who studies prehistoric fossil plants and animals.

Predator
An animal that hunts, kills, and eats other animals.

Puncture Wound
A hole through the skin and into the body of a living thing. A puncture wound can be caused by spikes, teeth, claws, or other kinds of weapons. If deep enough, the damage can be seen in the bone.

Scutes
Thick, bony plates that protect the bodies of armored dinosaurs. Scutes are still found today on the bodies of crocodiles and turtles.

Online Resources

Booklinks
NONFICTION NETWORK
FREE! ONLINE NONFICTION RESOURCES

To learn more about Xtreme Dinosaurs, visit abdobooklinks.com. These links are routinely monitored and updated to provide the most current information available.

INDEX

A
Allosaurus 10
ankylosaur 6, 7, 12, 13, 17, 21, 25, 29
Ankylosaurus 20, 21

C
carnivore 10
Colorado 27
cow 16
Cretaceous period 4

D
dog 14

E
Earth 28
Edmontonia 21
Euoplocephalus 4, 7

F
fossil 13, 18, 26, 27

G
gargoyle 24
Gargoyleosaurus 24, 25

H
herbivores 16

J
Jurassic period 4

L
Larson, Gary 11

M
Morrison Formation 27

N
nodosaur 21
North America 20, 23, 25

O
osteoderm 8

P
paleontologist 11, 26
puncture wound 10

S
Scutellosaurus 22, 23
scutes 6, 8, 22
Simmons, Thag 11
stegosaur 6, 8, 9, 10, 11, 16, 22
Stegosaurus 18, 19, 27

T
thagomizer 11
Thyreophorans 4

W
Wyoming 27